# QUANTUM COMPUTING
# FOR THE PRACTIAL MAN

## History, Current State,
## and
## Future Implications

BY

C.P. HOLGATE

2nd Edition 2025

# Table of Contents

# Index of Key Terms

# Chapter 1

## Classical Bits vs Quantum Bits (Qubits)

### Introduction

In classical computing, information is represented and processed using bits, the fundamental unit of digital data. Each bit holds a value of either 0 or 1. Classical computation is inherently deterministic, rooted in the binary logic of classical physics. In contrast, quantum computing introduces the concept of the qubit (quantum bit), which exists not only in the discrete states of 0 and 1 but also in any quantum superposition of these states. This unique property allows quantum computers to process information in ways that transcend classical limitations. This chapter explores these core distinctions, the physical and logical implementation of bits and qubits, and their implications for computation.

### Classical Bits

Classical bits are stored using macroscopic phenomena that can reliably assume one of two distinct states. For example:

- **Transistors**: Represent binary states via high or low voltage.

- **Magnetic storage**: Magnetized regions represent binary orientation.

- **Optical media**: Presence or absence of pits encodes digital data.

Classical computing systems manipulate bits using logic gates based on Boolean algebra. These gates include AND, OR, NOT, NAND, and XOR. Computations proceed through a sequence of these operations, executed by CPUs and digital circuits at blazing speeds. Although powerful, classical systems are ultimately limited by their reliance on sequential and deterministic logic.

**Diagram 1: Classical Logic Gate Diagram**

```
Input A ──┬──────────┐      Output = A AND B
     │ AND  ├─────────┴ 1 or 0
Input B ──┘      │
```

**Quantum Bits (Qubits)**

Qubits, unlike classical bits, exist in a quantum state defined by a linear combination of basis states $|0\rangle$ and $|1\rangle$

$|\psi\rangle = \alpha|0\rangle + \beta|1\rangle$ where $\alpha$ and $\beta$ are complex amplitudes, and $|\alpha|^2 + |\beta|^2 = 1$.

The coefficients $\alpha$ and $\beta$ determine the probabilities of measuring the qubit in state 0 or 1, respectively. Due to superposition, a qubit can encode more information than a classical bit. Moreover, multiple qubits can become **entangled**, creating correlations that persist even when the qubits are physically separated.

**Diagram 2: Bloch Sphere Representation of a Qubit**

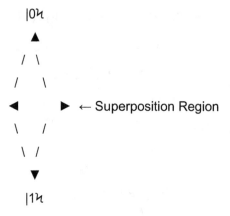

Entanglement and superposition are foundational to quantum computational advantage.

**Physical Implementation of Qubits**

Qubits are realized in physical systems where quantum effects are prominent. Each technology platform offers different benefits and constraints:

- **Superconducting Qubits**: Created using Josephson junctions on microchips, manipulated via microwave pulses.

- **Trapped Ion Qubits**: Atomic ions suspended in electromagnetic fields and controlled with laser pulses.

- **Photonic Qubits**: Encode information in the polarization or phase of individual photons.

- **Spin Qubits**: Electrons in quantum dots manipulated via magnetic resonance.

- **Nitrogen-Vacancy (NV) Centers**: Defects in diamonds that trap single electrons.

**Diagram 3: Example Physical Qubit Technologies**

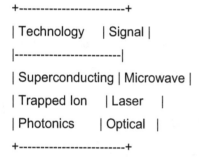

```
+------------------------+
| Technology    | Signal |
|------------------------|
| Superconducting | Microwave |
| Trapped Ion    | Laser   |
| Photonics      | Optical  |
+------------------------+
```

## Quantum Gates and Circuits

Quantum gates are unitary operations that manipulate qubit states while preserving quantum information. Unlike classical logic gates, quantum gates can create and manipulate superpositions and entanglements.

Examples:

- **Hadamard (H)**: Creates superposition: H|0⟩= (|0⟩+ | 1⟩)/√2

- **Pauli Gates (X, Y, Z)**: Quantum analogs of classical NOT, phase shifts.

- **CNOT (Controlled-NOT)**: A two-qubit gate that flips the target qubit based on the control qubit's value.

**Diagram 4: CNOT Gate Circuit**

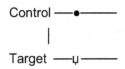

Control ——•————

Target ——ц————

Quantum circuits are built from sequences of gates, and can implement algorithms such as Shor's or Grover's.

**Storage and Computation Comparison**

| Property | Classical Bit | Quantum Bit (Qubit) |
|---|---|---|
| State | 0 or 1 | $\alpha$ \|0⟩ $+ \beta$ \|1⟩ (superposition) |
| Representation | Voltage, charge | Quantum state vector |
| Logic | Boolean logic | Quantum |

10

| | | |
|---|---|---|
| Operations | gates | unitary gates |
| Interconnection | Independent | Entangled with others |
| Copying Data | Clonable | No-cloning theorem |
| Measurement | Direct | Probabilistic, collapses |

## Computational Implications

Quantum computing enables massive parallelism by operating on a superposition of states. When applied to certain problems, this leads to exponential improvements in performance. Notably:

- **Shor's Algorithm**: Efficiently factors large integers, breaking RSA encryption.

- **Grover's Algorithm**: Speeds up unstructured search by a square root factor.

- **Quantum Simulation**: Accurately models quantum systems for chemistry and materials science.

However, the power of quantum computation is tempered by challenges such as:

- **Decoherence**: Qubits lose information due to interaction with the environment.

- **Quantum Error Correction**: Complex schemes are needed to preserve information.

- **Hardware Limitations**: Scalability and fidelity remain active research areas.

---

## Conclusion

The evolution from classical bits to qubits signals more than a technological shift—it marks a philosophical transformation in how we conceptualize computation and information. Qubits, with their probabilistic and entangled nature, unlock computational strategies beyond the reach of classical systems. As quantum technology matures, it holds the potential to redefine fields from cryptography to artificial intelligence, ushering in a new computational era.

- **Bit** – The smallest unit of data in classical computing, representing a value of 0 or 1.

- **Boolean Logic** – The system of logic used in classical computing, based on binary values and logical operations such as AND, OR, and NOT.

- **Qubit (Quantum Bit)** – A unit of quantum information that exists in a superposition of 0 and 1 states simultaneously.

- **Superposition** – A fundamental quantum principle where a qubit can exist in multiple states at once.

- **Entanglement** – A quantum phenomenon where two or more qubits become linked such that the state of one affects the state of the others.

- **Bloch Sphere** – A visual representation of a qubit's state in a three-dimensional space.

- **Hadamard Gate** – A quantum logic gate that puts a qubit into a superposition of 0 and 1.

- **CNOT Gate** – A quantum gate that flips a target qubit if the control qubit is in state 1.

- **Decoherence** – The process by which quantum information is lost to the environment, causing a qubit to lose its quantum behavior.

- **Quantum Error Correction** – Techniques used to protect quantum information from errors due to decoherence and other quantum noise.

- **No-Cloning Theorem** – A principle stating that it is impossible to create an identical copy of an arbitrary unknown quantum state.

# Glossary for Chapter 1

- **Bit:** Basic unit of information in classical computing, represented as either 0 or 1.

- **Qubit:** Quantum bit, the basic unit of quantum information, capable of existing in superposition states.

- **Superposition:** Quantum phenomenon where particles simultaneously exist in multiple states.

- **Entanglement:** Quantum phenomenon in which particle states become interdependent regardless of spatial separation.

- **Quantum Coherence:** Duration in which quantum states maintain their integrity without environmental interference.

- **Quantum Gates:** Quantum analogues to classical logic gates, used to manipulate qubit states.

# Chapter 2

# Historical Foundations of Quantum Computing

The historical foundations of quantum computing lie at the intersection of physics, mathematics, and computer science. They trace back to the early 20th century when the core principles of quantum mechanics were being formulated. Understanding this rich historical context is crucial to appreciating how quantum computing evolved from abstract theory to an emerging technological reality with profound implications for science and society.

### Early Quantum Mechanics and Theoretical Inspiration

Quantum computing's conceptual roots are grounded in the birth of quantum mechanics in the 1920s and 1930s. Pioneering scientists such as Max Planck, Niels Bohr, Werner Heisenberg, and Erwin Schrödinger laid down the foundational principles of the field—introducing the ideas of quantized energy levels, wave-particle duality, the uncertainty principle, and the probabilistic nature of quantum states. These ideas challenged classical mechanics and offered a radically new way of understanding physical phenomena at the atomic and subatomic levels.

15

**Diagram 1: Timeline of Early Quantum Discoveries**

1900   Planck's Quantization

1925   Heisenberg's Matrix Mechanics

1926   Schrödinger's Wave Mechanics

1935   Einstein-Podolsky-Rosen Paradox

These discoveries sparked philosophical debates about determinism and the completeness of quantum theory, most famously exemplified by the Einstein-Bohr debates.

**From Quantum Theory to Quantum Computation**

As researchers delved deeper into the quantum realm, they encountered properties like superposition and entanglement —concepts that would later prove central to quantum information theory. The departure from classical determinism led thinkers to explore how quantum behaviors could be applied to information processing. Physicist Richard Feynman, in the 1960s and 1970s, was among the first to propose that quantum mechanics might allow for fundamentally new ways of computing. He argued that simulating quantum systems on classical machines was inefficient, and that only a computer based on quantum rules could efficiently replicate these systems.

In 1982, Feynman formally introduced the idea of quantum computing in a lecture at MIT. He envisioned a new kind of computational device—one that used quantum properties to simulate other quantum systems. This notion represented a major conceptual leap, highlighting a new class of problems that classical computers could not efficiently solve.

David Deutsch of Oxford University extended Feynman's idea by defining a formal model of quantum computation. In 1985, he introduced the concept of a quantum Turing machine, laying the theoretical groundwork for quantum computation as a general-purpose method of information processing. Deutsch's work showed that quantum systems could perform any task a classical computer could—and more efficiently in certain cases.

**Diagram 2: Classical vs. Quantum Turing Machine (Conceptual)**

Classical TM:   Tape + Head + Finite State Machine
Quantum TM:    Tape + Superposition + Reversible Operations

His concept of quantum parallelism, where a quantum system could evaluate multiple inputs simultaneously due to superposition, opened the door to revolutionary advances in computational theory. It was now clear that quantum computing was not just an interesting theoretical possibility, but a potentially transformative computational paradigm.

---

## Breakthrough Algorithms and Practical Motivation

The 1990s saw the emergence of quantum algorithms that demonstrated real computational advantages. In 1994, Peter Shor developed a polynomial-time algorithm for integer factorization—an exponential improvement over the best classical algorithms. Shor's algorithm showed that quantum computers could break widely used public-key cryptosystems like RSA, highlighting the field's practical significance.

Shortly afterward, Lov Grover introduced an algorithm in 1996 that provided a quadratic speedup for searching unsorted databases. Grover's algorithm underscored that quantum computing offered more than just niche applications; it had the potential to speed up a broad range of problems in computer science, optimization, and artificial intelligence.

**Diagram 3: Algorithm Speedup Comparison**

Task: Factor a large number
Classical: $O(\exp(n))$
Quantum (Shor): $O(n^3)$

Task: Unstructured search
Classical: $O(n)$
Quantum (Grover): $O(\sqrt{n})$

These discoveries ignited global interest in quantum computing and catalyzed the formation of a new interdisciplinary research field. They also revealed the practical stakes involved in quantum computing—ranging from cryptography and national security to material science and artificial intelligence.

**Experimental Milestones and Technological Progress**

Following these theoretical advances, experimental physicists worked to demonstrate quantum computing in the lab. Techniques such as nuclear magnetic resonance (NMR), ion traps, and superconducting circuits enabled early demonstrations of quantum gates and algorithms using a small number of qubits.

In 2001, IBM and Stanford successfully demonstrated Shor's algorithm using a seven-qubit NMR quantum computer. Although limited in scale, this experiment was a significant milestone: it proved that quantum algorithms could be physically implemented, and it validated key principles in quantum computation.

The 2000s and 2010s saw rapid improvements in hardware platforms. Superconducting qubits, developed by IBM, Google, and others, became the leading architecture due to their scalability and integration with classical electronics. Trapped-ion systems demonstrated high coherence and precision, offering an alternative path toward large-scale quantum processors.

During this time, **D-Wave** introduced a commercial quantum annealing system, sparking debate about the definition and limits of quantum computation. Meanwhile, companies like **Rigetti**, **IonQ**, and **Xanadu** began exploring novel approaches using photonics, neutral atoms, and hybrid architectures.

## Institutional Support and the Modern Era

By the late 2010s, governments around the world began investing heavily in quantum computing. The U.S. National Quantum Initiative Act of 2018 established a coordinated national strategy, investing in quantum education, infrastructure, and industrial partnerships. Similar initiatives emerged in the European Union, China, Canada, and Australia, reflecting a growing recognition of quantum computing as a strategic frontier.

At the same time, academic programs in quantum computing expanded, with universities launching new degree offerings and interdisciplinary research centers. Private industry played a key role, with companies developing cloud-accessible quantum computers, open-source software toolkits, and training resources for quantum developers.

This ecosystem has matured rapidly, with quantum computing now positioned as a high-priority technology for economic competitiveness, national security, and scientific leadership.

## The Path Forward

As we move deeper into the era of Noisy Intermediate-Scale Quantum (NISQ) devices, quantum computers with 50 to several hundred qubits are becoming available. While still error-prone and limited in scope, these devices can tackle specialized problems in quantum chemistry, materials science, and machine learning that challenge classical supercomputers.

The journey from foundational physics to practical computing marks one of the most remarkable scientific transformations of the modern age. With sustained research, interdisciplinary collaboration, and ethical foresight, quantum computing is poised to reshape how we compute, understand, and interact with the world around us.

### Diagram 4: Evolution of Quantum Computing Milestones

| | |
|---|---|
| 1900s | Quantum Theory |
| 1980s | Concept of Quantum Computers |
| 1990s | Quantum Algorithms |
| 2000s | Experimental Devices |
| 2020s | Cloud Quantum Platforms |

As we move deeper into the era of Noisy Intermediate-Scale Quantum (NISQ) devices, quantum computers with 50 to several hundred qubits are becoming available. While still error-prone and limited in scope, these devices can tackle specialized problems in quantum chemistry, materials science, and machine learning that challenge classical supercomputers.

The journey from foundational physics to practical computing marks one of the most remarkable scientific transformations of the modern age. With sustained research, interdisciplinary collaboration, and ethical foresight, quantum computing is poised to reshape how we compute, understand, and interact with the world around us.

## Glossary for Chapter 2

- **Quantum Mechanics** – A fundamental theory in physics that describes nature at the smallest scales of energy levels of atoms and subatomic particles.

- **Superposition** – A quantum principle allowing a qubit to be in a combination of the |0⟩and |1⟩states simultaneously.

- **Entanglement** – A quantum phenomenon where qubits become interconnected such that the state of one instantly influences the state of another, regardless of distance.

- **Quantum Turing Machine** – A theoretical model of a

quantum computer extending the classical Turing machine to operate with quantum states and unitary transformations.

- **Quantum Parallelism** – The ability of a quantum system to process multiple inputs or paths simultaneously through superposition.

- **Shor's Algorithm** – A quantum algorithm capable of factoring large integers exponentially faster than the best-known classical methods.

- **Grover's Algorithm** – A quantum search algorithm that provides quadratic speedup over classical methods for unstructured search problems.

- **Noisy Intermediate-Scale Quantum (NISQ)** – A term for the current generation of quantum computers that have enough qubits to perform meaningful tasks but are limited by noise and error rates.

- **Quantum Supremacy** – The point at which a quantum computer can perform a computation that is infeasible for any classical computer in a reasonable time.

- **Quantum Simulation** – The use of quantum computers to simulate complex quantum systems that are difficult to model on classical computers.

# Chapter 3

# Quantum Algorithms and Their Development

## Introduction

Quantum algorithms leverage the principles of quantum mechanics—such as superposition, entanglement, and interference—to outperform their classical counterparts in specific problem domains. This chapter explores the foundational algorithms in quantum computing, their computational advantages, and how they are constructed and executed within quantum circuits.

---

## The Structure of Quantum Algorithms

Quantum algorithms are typically structured into three key stages:

1. **Initialization** – Qubits are prepared in a known state, usually $|0\rangle$

2. **Quantum Transformation** – Quantum gates are applied to create superpositions, entangle qubits, and

evolve the system.

3. **Measurement** – The quantum state is measured, collapsing superpositions and producing a classical result.

These stages allow quantum computers to explore many possible solutions in parallel and extract meaningful results with fewer steps than classical computers for specific tasks.

---

### Shor's Algorithm: Factoring Integers

Peter Shor's algorithm (1994) demonstrated that quantum computers can factor large integers exponentially faster than classical algorithms. The algorithm is used to solve the problem of period finding, a key step in breaking RSA encryption.

### Diagram 1: Shor's Algorithm Workflow

Classical Input → Quantum Fourier Transform → Period Finding → Classical Post-Processing → Factors

Key Steps:

- Use quantum parallelism to evaluate a modular exponential function.

- Apply the quantum Fourier transform to detect

periodicity.

- Use the period to determine the prime factors.

Shor's algorithm runs in polynomial time, threatening current cryptographic systems based on factoring.

---

## Grover's Algorithm: Database Search

Grover's algorithm (1996) solves the problem of searching an unsorted database in $O(\sqrt{n})$ time, providing a quadratic speedup over classical algorithms.

### Diagram 2: Grover's Algorithm Concept

Initial State → Oracle Marking → Amplitude Amplification → Measurement → Desired Item

Key Components:

- **Oracle**: Marks the correct solution by flipping its phase.

- **Diffusion Operator**: Amplifies the probability amplitude of the correct state.

Grover's algorithm is useful in optimization, constraint satisfaction, and AI search problems.

---

## Quantum Fourier Transform (QFT)

The quantum Fourier transform is a central component of many quantum algorithms, including Shor's. It transforms quantum amplitudes to reveal periodicity in the data.

Mathematically, the QFT transforms a quantum state from the computational basis to the frequency basis, analogous to the classical discrete Fourier transform but executed in $O(n^2)$ time on a quantum computer.

---

## Quantum Phase Estimation (QPE)

Quantum phase estimation is a subroutine used in algorithms like Shor's and for calculating eigenvalues of unitary operators. It enables a quantum computer to estimate the phase $\theta$ in the equation $U|\psi\rangle = e^{(2\pi i \theta)}|\psi\rangle$

Applications include:

- Solving linear systems

- Hamiltonian simulation

- Quantum chemistry problems

## Amplitude Amplification and Variants

Generalizing Grover's algorithm, amplitude amplification can be used in a wider range of algorithms to boost the likelihood of desired outcomes. It is used in quantum counting and quantum walk algorithms.

### Diagram 3: Amplitude Amplification Cycle

$|\psi\rangle \rightarrow$ Oracle $\rightarrow$ Reflect about mean $\rightarrow$ Repeat $\rightarrow$ Measure

## Variational Quantum Algorithms (VQAs)

VQAs use parameterized quantum circuits combined with classical optimization loops. Examples include:

- **VQE (Variational Quantum Eigensolver)**: Estimates the ground-state energy of a Hamiltonian.

- **QAOA (Quantum Approximate Optimization Algorithm)**: Solves combinatorial optimization problems.

These algorithms are suitable for NISQ-era devices.

---

## Quantum Walk Algorithms

Quantum walks are the quantum analog of classical random

walks and serve as the basis for several algorithms, including search and graph traversal. They offer exponential or polynomial speedups depending on the structure of the problem space.

## Summary

Quantum algorithms mark a radical departure from classical paradigms, enabling solutions to previously intractable problems. Foundational algorithms like Shor's and Grover's illustrate how quantum mechanics can be applied to computational tasks. As quantum hardware evolves, a growing set of algorithms is emerging, tailored for both near-term and long-term devices.

# Glossary for Chapter 3

- **Quantum Algorithm** – A sequence of quantum operations designed to solve a problem more efficiently than classical methods.

- **Shor's Algorithm** – A quantum algorithm for factoring large numbers exponentially faster than classical algorithms.

- **Grover's Algorithm** – A quantum search algorithm providing quadratic speedup for unstructured data search.

- **Quantum Fourier Transform (QFT)** – A quantum version of the discrete Fourier transform, essential for periodicity detection.

- **Oracle** – A black-box function used to identify correct solutions in search problems.

- **Amplitude Amplification** – A technique that increases the probability of measuring the correct solution.

- **Quantum Phase Estimation (QPE)** – An algorithm to estimate eigenvalues (phases) of unitary operators.

- **Variational Quantum Algorithm (VQA)** – A hybrid quantum-classical algorithm using parameter optimization.

- **VQE (Variational Quantum Eigensolver)** – An algorithm for estimating the lowest eigenvalue of a Hamiltonian.

- **QAOA (Quantum Approximate Optimization Algorithm)** – A variational algorithm for solving combinatorial problems.

- **Quantum Walk** – A quantum analog of a classical random walk, used in search and graph-based algorithms.

# Chapter 4
# Quantum Hardware and Architecture

## Introduction

Quantum hardware lies at the heart of all quantum computing efforts, serving as the physical foundation on which quantum operations are performed. Unlike classical hardware that manipulates binary bits, quantum hardware must support the delicate quantum states of qubits. In this chapter, we explore major quantum hardware platforms, key components of quantum architecture, challenges in engineering scalable systems, and the trade-offs involved in competing technologies.

---

## Major Quantum Hardware Platforms

Different research teams and companies use varied technologies to realize qubits, each with unique advantages and constraints. The most prevalent hardware platforms include:

- **Superconducting Qubits**: Fabricated using Josephson junctions; used by IBM, Google, and Rigetti.

- **Trapped Ion Qubits**: Use individual ions suspended

in electromagnetic traps; favored by IonQ and Honeywell.

- **Photonic Qubits**: Use light particles (photons) with encoding via polarization or time bins.

- **Spin Qubits**: Use the spin state of electrons in quantum dots.

- **Neutral Atoms**: Use cold atoms in optical lattices controlled by lasers.

## Diagram 1: Comparison of Quantum Hardware Platforms

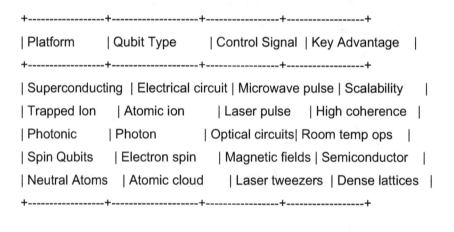

| Platform | Qubit Type | Control Signal | Key Advantage |
|---|---|---|---|
| Superconducting | Electrical circuit | Microwave pulse | Scalability |
| Trapped Ion | Atomic ion | Laser pulse | High coherence |
| Photonic | Photon | Optical circuits | Room temp ops |
| Spin Qubits | Electron spin | Magnetic fields | Semiconductor |
| Neutral Atoms | Atomic cloud | Laser tweezers | Dense lattices |

## Qubit Initialization, Manipulation, and Measurement

Quantum circuits begin with qubit initialization, usually into the |0⟩ state. Manipulations are done through sequences of quantum gates, and the process concludes with qubit measurement, collapsing the quantum state to classical bits.

## Diagram 2: Lifecycle of a Qubit

|0⟩Initialization → Gate Operations → Entanglement →
Readout (|0⟩or |1⟩)

Each operation must be executed with extreme precision.
Any interaction with the environment risks decoherence.

---

## Architecture and Qubit Connectivity

In practical devices, qubits are laid out in 1D, 2D, or 3D
architectures. Qubit connectivity—the ability for qubits to
interact—significantly influences algorithm efficiency.

- **Nearest-neighbor**: Qubits only interact with adjacent
  partners (e.g., grid layout).

- **All-to-all**: Any qubit can interact with any other
  (common in ion traps).

## Diagram 3: Qubit Connectivity Models

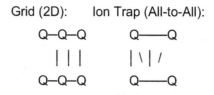

---

## Error Correction and Fault Tolerance

Quantum systems are error-prone due to decoherence and gate imperfections. To achieve fault-tolerant computation, quantum error correction (QEC) schemes such as the **surface code** are employed.

Key terms:

- **Fidelity**: Probability that a gate or qubit behaves as expected.

- **Error Threshold**: The max allowable error rate before QEC fails.

- **Logical Qubit**: Encoded from multiple physical qubits to resist errors.

**Diagram 4: Logical vs. Physical Qubit** Logical Qubit = Encoded State using 9 Physical Qubits

(e.g., Shor Code)

---

## Cryogenic and Control Infrastructure

Most quantum processors require cryogenic systems to maintain low temperatures (millikelvin scale), reducing thermal noise and preserving coherence. Control electronics operate classical-quantum interfaces:

- **Control lines**: Deliver microwave or laser pulses.

- **Readout lines**: Retrieve measurement signals.

- **Amplifiers**: Boost faint signals from the qubit system.

---

## Hybrid Quantum-Classical Architectures

In the NISQ era, quantum processors are often coupled with classical CPUs and GPUs. Hybrid models allow for preprocessing, optimization, and post-processing of quantum operations.

- **VQE and QAOA** algorithms use this model.

- **Cloud quantum platforms** enable access to remote quantum hardware.

### Diagram 5: Hybrid Quantum-Classical Workflow

Classical CPU ↔ Quantum Processor ↔ Cloud Interface

---

## Conclusion

Quantum hardware is advancing rapidly through multiple competing architectures. The success of quantum computing depends not only on increasing the number of qubits but on improving fidelity, connectivity, and error correction. As engineers build increasingly sophisticated quantum machines, innovations in architecture, materials science, and cryogenic control will continue to shape the trajectory of this revolutionary field.

---

## Glossary for Chapter 4

- **Superconducting Qubits** – Qubits based on circuits that exhibit zero electrical resistance at low temperatures, enabling stable quantum states.

- **Trapped Ion Qubits** – Qubits formed by isolating and manipulating individual ions using electromagnetic fields in a vacuum.

- **Photonic Qubits** – Qubits encoded in the quantum states of light particles, such as polarization or phase.

- **Cryogenic Systems** – Low-temperature environments essential for maintaining coherence in superconducting quantum processors.

- **Quantum Coherence** – The ability of a quantum system to maintain superposition over time, critical for reliable computation.

- **Quantum Gate** – The basic unit of quantum operations that alters the state of qubits, similar to classical logic gates.

- **Fidelity** – A measure of how accurately a quantum operation or gate is performed.

- **Scalability** – The capability of a quantum architecture to increase the number of qubits and operations without significant loss of performance.

# Chapter 5

# Quantum Software and Programming Frameworks

## Introduction

While quantum hardware is essential for running quantum computations, software frameworks and programming environments play a pivotal role in enabling algorithm development, control, and execution. This chapter examines major quantum programming languages, software development kits (SDKs), and how they interact with quantum hardware. We explore low-level gate-based programming, high-level abstractions, and hybrid workflows involving classical and quantum resources.

---

## Quantum Programming Models

Quantum software is organized around several models that guide how developers interact with qubits:

- **Gate-based (circuit) model**: Dominant paradigm involving direct programming of qubit gates.

- **Measurement-based model**: Computation is performed via sequences of qubit measurements.

- **Adiabatic model**: Used in quantum annealers; slowly evolves the system into the problem's solution.

- **Hybrid quantum-classical models**: Combine quantum circuits with classical optimization (e.g., VQE, QAOA).

## Diagram 1: Quantum Programming Models Overview

Gate-based —▶ Unitary Circuits

Measurement-based —▶ Cluster State Logic

Adiabatic —▶ Quantum Annealing

Hybrid —▶ Variational Algorithms

---

## Key Programming Frameworks

Quantum software frameworks provide tools, libraries, and simulators that let users build and run quantum algorithms:

- **Qiskit** (IBM): Open-source SDK with Python API, gate-level control, and simulators.

- **Cirq** (Google): Designed for noisy intermediate-scale quantum (NISQ) devices with emphasis on circuit design.

- **QuTiP**: Quantum Toolbox in Python, useful for simulating open quantum systems.

- **PennyLane**: Supports hybrid quantum-classical workflows; integrates with PyTorch and TensorFlow.

- **Forest SDK** (Rigetti): Includes Quil language, pyQuil API, and the Quilc compiler.

- **Strawberry Fields** (Xanadu): Specialized for photonic quantum computing.

## Diagram 2: Comparison of Quantum SDKs

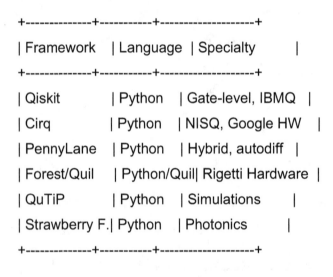

```
+--------------+-----------+--------------------+
| Framework    | Language  | Specialty          |
+--------------+-----------+--------------------+
| Qiskit       | Python    | Gate-level, IBMQ   |
| Cirq         | Python    | NISQ, Google HW    |
| PennyLane    | Python    | Hybrid, autodiff   |
| Forest/Quil  | Python/Quil| Rigetti Hardware  |
| QuTiP        | Python    | Simulations        |
| Strawberry F.| Python    | Photonics          |
+--------------+-----------+--------------------+
```

## Quantum Programming Languages

Quantum languages differ in abstraction levels:

- **High-level**: Python-based, developer-friendly (Qiskit, Cirq)

- **Intermediate**: Quil, OpenQASM (assembly-like syntax)

- **Low-level**: Native pulse-level control for hardware calibration

Open standards like **OpenQASM** aim to unify gate-level programming across platforms, supporting portability and interoperability.

---

## Compilers and Optimization Tools

Compilers translate quantum programs into sequences of hardware-specific instructions. Key tasks include:

- **Gate synthesis**: Expressing high-level gates with supported primitives.

- **Mapping and routing**: Aligning logical qubits to physical layout constraints.

- **Error mitigation**: Inserting noise-aware operations to reduce decoherence impact.

**Diagram 3: Quantum Compilation Process**

Algorithm → Gate Decomposition → Mapping to Qubits → Optimization → Executable

---

## Simulation and Emulation

Before running algorithms on real hardware, developers use simulators to verify correctness and estimate performance:

- **State-vector simulators**: Model quantum states exactly (limited by qubit count).

- **Stabilizer simulators**: Efficiently simulate specific quantum states.

- **Noise-aware simulators**: Include decoherence and gate error models.

Simulators are critical for debugging, testing, and validating new algorithms.

---

## Hybrid and Cloud Environments

Hybrid workflows allow real-time collaboration between quantum and classical systems. Users can:

- Optimize variational parameters with classical loops.

- Access remote hardware via **IBM Quantum, Amazon Braket, Azure Quantum**, and **Google Quantum AI**.

## Challenges and Future Directions

Key challenges in quantum software development include:

- **Scalability**: Managing circuits with hundreds of qubits.

- **Abstraction**: Building reusable quantum libraries and high-level languages.

- **Toolchain unification**: Standardizing across platforms.

Emerging directions involve:

- **Quantum IDEs**: Integrated environments with visualization and debugging tools.

- **Auto-coding**: AI-generated quantum programs based on problem statements.

---

## Conclusion

Quantum software frameworks are rapidly evolving to meet the demands of increasingly powerful quantum devices. By enabling algorithm development, circuit optimization, simulation, and integration with classical systems, they form the bridge between theoretical potential and practical application.

As software matures alongside hardware, it will accelerate the transition from experimental quantum computing to scalable real-world solutions.

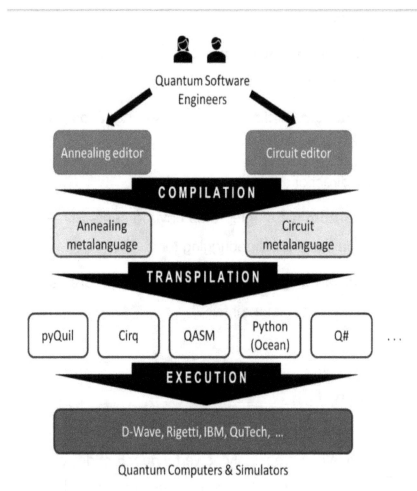

Quantum Computers & Simulators

# Glossary for Chapter 5

- **Quantum Programming Language:** A language developed for expressing and executing quantum computations.

- **Quantum Simulator:** A classical computing system that mimics quantum operations to test and debug quantum algorithms.

- **Cloud-Based Quantum Computing:** Accessing and operating quantum processors via internet-connected platforms.

- **Quantum Error Correction:** Techniques for identifying and correcting errors in quantum state manipulation and computation.

- **Hybrid Quantum-Classical Systems:** Architectures that combine quantum computing power with classical computing systems to solve complex problems.

- **Quantum Middleware:** Software that facilitates interaction between quantum applications and hardware resources.

- **Quantum SDK (Software Development Kit):** A suite of tools and libraries for quantum programming and algorithm development.

# Chapter 6

# Current Status and Achievements in Quantum Computing

## Introduction

Quantum computing has evolved from theoretical constructs and laboratory demonstrations into a rapidly advancing field marked by significant technological milestones. While fully fault-tolerant, large-scale quantum computers are still on the horizon, many noteworthy achievements have been made in the current era—referred to as the Noisy Intermediate-Scale Quantum (NISQ) era. This chapter explores the status of quantum computing as of today, highlights major breakthroughs, and evaluates practical applications underway or emerging.

## The NISQ Era and Its Characteristics

The term **NISQ** (Noisy Intermediate-Scale Quantum), coined by John Preskill, describes the current generation of quantum processors, which typically possess 50–500 qubits. These machines:

- Are prone to noise and decoherence

- Lack full error correction

- Can execute quantum algorithms of limited depth

- Are suitable for exploratory and hybrid quantum-classical algorithms

**Diagram 1: Quantum Computing Maturity Curve**

| Classical → NISQ → Fault-Tolerant → Quantum Advantage → Ubiquity

NISQ devices are enabling researchers to understand system behavior, optimize hybrid workflows, and identify benchmarks for future platforms.

---

**Quantum Supremacy Milestones**

In 2019, Google announced it had achieved **quantum supremacy**—a point where a quantum computer solved a problem faster than the best classical supercomputer could. Their 53-qubit Sycamore processor completed a random circuit sampling task in 200 seconds, a computation that would take a classical supercomputer 10,000 years.

Subsequent efforts by IBM and Chinese research groups have added more evidence that quantum processors can perform tasks outside classical reach, albeit for specialized problems with limited practical use.

---

## Commercial Hardware Development

One of the most novel approaches in quantum hardware comes from **Microsoft**, which is investing in **topological quantum computing**. This approach aims to achieve fault tolerance and long coherence times through a fundamentally different type of qubit—the **topological qubit**.

**Topological qubits** rely on **non-Abelian anyons**, exotic quasiparticles whose quantum states depend on their braiding paths through spacetime. Instead of storing information in a fragile state, topological qubits store it in the global properties of the system, which are highly resistant to local disturbances. This offers potential for intrinsic error resilience.

Microsoft's architecture uses **Majorana zero modes**—hypothetical particles predicted to exist at the edges of certain superconducting materials. If realized experimentally, they could form the basis for topological qubits that are naturally protected against decoherence.

**Diagram: Concept of Topological Qubit Stability**

Majorana A●————————————●Majorana B

| Braiding Path → Error-Protected State

Logical qubit encoded in spatial configuration, not local state.

This approach remains in the research phase, but Microsoft's commitment to topological qubits reflects a long-term strategy aimed at building scalable, fault-tolerant quantum computers from the ground up.

Several companies have developed working quantum hardware available via the cloud or on-premises integration:

- **IBM Quantum**: Offers superconducting qubit systems up to 127 qubits (Eagle processor) with roadmaps extending to 1,000+ qubits.

- **IonQ**: Uses trapped-ion technology with high-fidelity gates and all-to-all connectivity.

- **Google Quantum AI**: Developing Sycamore successors with error mitigation strategies.

- **Rigetti, Xanadu, D-Wave**: Each focusing on superconducting, photonic, and annealing approaches respectively.

**Diagram 2: Current Qubit Counts by Vendor**

IBM : 127 (Eagle)

IonQ : ~32

Google : 72 (Bristlecone)

Rigetti : ~80

D-Wave : 5000 (Quantum Annealer)

---

## Cloud Quantum Platforms

Major cloud providers are making quantum resources accessible to developers, educators, and researchers globally:

- **IBM Quantum Experience**

- **Amazon Braket**

- **Microsoft Azure Quantum**

- **Google Cloud Quantum Computing Service**

These platforms provide simulators, device access, and SDKs like Qiskit, PennyLane, and Cirq.

## Benchmarks and Performance Metrics

Assessing quantum computers involves metrics such as:

- **Qubit coherence time**: Duration a qubit retains its quantum state.

- **Gate fidelity**: Accuracy of quantum gate operations.

- **Quantum volume**: A holistic metric evaluating number of qubits, error rates, and gate depth.

- **Crosstalk**: Unwanted interactions between qubits during multi-qubit operations.

## Diagram 3: Quantum Volume Comparison (Sample Illustration)

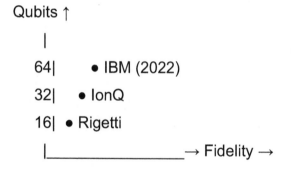

```
Qubits ↑
   |
 64|      • IBM (2022)
 32|    • IonQ
 16| • Rigetti
   |_____→ Fidelity →
```

**Emerging Applications in Practice**

Though general-purpose quantum computing is years away, several practical areas are being explored:

- **Quantum Chemistry**: Simulating molecules for materials science and pharmaceuticals.

- **Optimization**: Using VQE and QAOA for logistics, finance, and machine learning tasks.

- **Quantum Machine Learning (QML)**: Applying quantum kernels or classifiers in hybrid AI systems.

- **Secure Communication**: Integrating quantum key distribution with classical networks.

---

**Open Challenges**

Current limitations include:

- **Scalability**: Building large-scale systems with fault tolerance.

- **Error Correction**: Implementing surface codes or other QEC strategies reliably.

- **Standardization**: Developing protocols, file formats, and cross-vendor tools.

- **Energy Use**: Cryogenics and control electronics require significant power and infrastructure.

## Conclusion

Quantum computing has made substantial strides, transitioning from conceptual prototypes to publicly accessible platforms. While today's systems remain constrained by noise and scale, they are powerful testbeds for developing future technologies. The NISQ era is not the end goal but an important stepping stone to a fault-tolerant, quantum-enhanced future.

---

# Glossary for Chapter 6

- **NISQ (Noisy Intermediate-Scale Quantum)** – Quantum processors with tens to hundreds of qubits, prone to noise, and lacking full error correction.

- **Quantum Supremacy** – The point at which a

quantum computer performs a task beyond the capability of classical computers.

- **Quantum Volume** – A metric developed by IBM to assess a quantum computer's overall capability.

- **Qubit Coherence Time** – The time during which a qubit can maintain its quantum state.

- **Gate Fidelity** – A measure of how accurately a quantum gate performs the intended transformation.

- **Crosstalk** – Interference between qubits that leads to errors during multi-qubit operations.

- **Surface Code** – A leading quantum error correction method based on 2D qubit layouts.

- **QAOA (Quantum Approximate Optimization Algorithm)** – A variational algorithm useful in solving optimization problems on NISQ devices.

- **QKD (Quantum Key Distribution)** – A method of secure communication using quantum principles to share encryption keys.

- **Quantum Volume Benchmarking** – A method to evaluate how well a quantum processor can run complex quantum circuits.

# Chapter 7

# Quantum Computing and the Future of Cryptography and Security

## Introduction

Quantum computing presents both a challenge and an opportunity to the field of information security. On one hand, powerful quantum algorithms threaten to break widely used encryption methods. On the other, quantum principles such as entanglement and uncertainty enable new paradigms for secure communication. This chapter explores how quantum computing is reshaping the future of cryptography and digital security, including the impact on blockchain technology and the transition to post-quantum cryptography.

---

## The Threat to Classical Cryptography

Modern cryptographic systems rely on mathematical problems that are computationally hard for classical computers to solve. Notably:

- **RSA** depends on the difficulty of factoring large

integers.

- **ECC (Elliptic Curve Cryptography)** depends on solving the elliptic curve discrete logarithm problem.

- **Diffie-Hellman** relies on the difficulty of computing discrete logarithms.

**Shor's algorithm**, a quantum algorithm, can solve both factoring and discrete logarithms in polynomial time, thereby compromising the foundational assumptions of these systems.

**Diagram 1: Impact of Shor's Algorithm**

Classical Hard Problem → RSA / ECC / DH → Quantum Computer + Shor → Decryption of Encrypted Data

**Post-Quantum Cryptography (PQC)**

PQC involves developing cryptographic algorithms resistant to attacks from quantum computers. These algorithms rely on mathematical problems thought to be hard for both classical and quantum systems, such as:

- **Lattice-based cryptography**

- **Code-based cryptography**

- **Multivariate polynomial equations**

- **Hash-based signatures**

The U.S. National Institute of Standards and Technology (NIST) is leading a standardization process for PQC algorithms.

**Diagram 2: Timeline for Post-Quantum Transition**

2020: NIST PQC Project Launched

2024: Finalists Announced

2025–2030: Gradual Adoption in Software and Hardware Systems

**Quantum Key Distribution (QKD)**

QKD offers an entirely new model of secure key exchange, grounded in quantum mechanics rather than computational hardness. It enables two parties to generate a shared encryption key using entangled photons. If an eavesdropper tries to intercept the key, the act of measurement alters the system, revealing the intrusion.

QKD protocols include:

- **BB84** (Bennett and Brassard, 1984)

- **E91** (Ekert, 1991)

Limitations:

- Requires specialized hardware

- Distance and speed limitations

- Vulnerability to implementation flaws

**Diagram 3: BB84 Protocol Concept**

Alice → Encodes Photons → Sends → Bob → Measures → Compare Bases → Keep Matching Bits → Key

---

**Blockchain and Quantum Risks**

Blockchain networks rely on cryptographic principles for consensus, immutability, and digital signatures. However, the very properties that make blockchain secure in the classical era become its weaknesses in a quantum world. These include:

- **Digital Signatures**: Most blockchain systems use elliptic curve cryptography (e.g., ECDSA in Bitcoin). Shor's algorithm can break these systems, allowing attackers to forge transactions and potentially rewrite blockchain history.

- **Proof-of-Work Security**: Mining competition is based on hashing algorithms that quantum computers could potentially accelerate via Grover's algorithm, reducing mining difficulty.

- **Key Recovery from Public Keys**: In many blockchains, public keys are exposed during transaction broadcasts. A quantum attacker could retroactively derive private keys, compromising funds.

**Diagram 4: Quantum Threat to Blockchain Integrity**

Block Signature → Vulnerable to Shor's Algorithm Quantum Breakthrough → Replay Attacks / Forged Transactions

Additionally, quantum computing could eliminate the need for large prime numbers in encryption. Classical cryptography relies heavily on problems like prime factorization, assumed to be hard. Quantum computers efficiently solve these problems, making large prime numbers obsolete for securing digital information. The ability to factor large primes in polynomial time undermines the mathematical hardness that classical cryptographic systems depend on.

This capability not only affects existing encryption schemes like RSA but also calls into question the entire foundation of classical digital trust models—including blockchain. If signatures can be broken and transaction authenticity undermined, then the decentralized, trustless nature of blockchain becomes invalidated. In this scenario, blockchain may become obsolete unless fully quantum-resistant protocols are adopted.

Researchers and technologists are now exploring:

- Quantum-safe consensus mechanisms

- Quantum signature schemes (e.g., hash-based or lattice-based)

- Entanglement-enabled distributed ledgers

Without proactive quantum integration, blockchain systems face existential risk in the quantum era.

---

## Quantum-Safe Strategy and Migration

Security agencies and enterprises are now drafting roadmaps for transitioning to quantum-safe infrastructure:

- Inventory current cryptographic systems

- Evaluate vulnerability timelines

- Adopt PQC libraries and APIs

- Prepare for regulatory changes and compliance

Key organizations include:

- NIST (USA)

- ETSI (Europe)

- ANSSI (France)

- NSA (Quantum-Resistant Algorithms Program)

---

## Conclusion

The coming of quantum computing signals a tectonic shift in cybersecurity. It demands proactive planning, innovation in cryptographic systems, and international collaboration. While quantum poses threats to traditional systems, it also paves the way for fundamentally secure communication and identity protocols. Preparedness today ensures resilience tomorrow.

## Glossary for Chapter 7

- **Post-Quantum Cryptography (PQC)** –
  Cryptographic techniques designed to remain secure
  against both classical and quantum computer-based
  attacks.

- **Shor's Algorithm** – A quantum algorithm capable of
  factoring large integers and solving discrete
  logarithms, thereby breaking RSA and ECC.

- **Quantum Key Distribution (QKD)** – A method of
  secure key sharing that leverages quantum
  mechanics to detect eavesdropping.

- **BB84 Protocol** – The original QKD protocol using
  photon polarization to securely transmit encryption
  keys.

- **Lattice-Based Cryptography** – A class of
  cryptographic methods relying on lattice problems
  considered hard even for quantum computers.

- **ECDSA (Elliptic Curve Digital Signature
  Algorithm)** – A cryptographic algorithm used in
  blockchain systems, vulnerable to quantum attacks.

- **Hybrid Cryptography** – The combination of classical cryptographic methods with quantum-safe algorithms for a transitional phase.

- **Quantum-Resistant Blockchain** – Blockchain protocols designed with cryptographic primitives that are secure against quantum adversaries.

- **NSA Post-Quantum Guidance** – Recommendations and strategies issued by the U.S. National Security Agency for transitioning to quantum-safe algorithms.

- **Quantum-Safe Migration** – The phased approach of assessing and replacing current cryptographic systems to ensure resistance to quantum threats.

- **Quantum Authentication** – Use of quantum mechanisms such as entangled states to verify the identity of communicating parties.

- **Zero-Knowledge Proofs (ZKPs)** – Cryptographic protocols where one party proves knowledge of a secret without revealing it, increasingly relevant in quantum blockchain solutions.

- **Blind Quantum Computing** – A method allowing users to outsource quantum computations to a server without revealing the input, computation, or output.

- **Quantum-Secure Multiparty Computation** – A privacy-preserving protocol resistant to quantum adversaries, enabling joint computation without revealing private inputs.

- **Post-Quantum VPN** – A virtual private network that uses PQC algorithms to protect data traffic against future quantum attacks.

# Chapter 8

# Quantum Computing in Industry and Business Applications

Quantum computing has moved beyond the realm of research laboratories and theoretical academia into the dynamic environment of real-world industry applications. Across a variety of sectors, businesses are beginning to explore and experiment with the potential quantum advantage—leveraging quantum algorithms and hybrid architectures to solve problems that are intractable for classical computers. From portfolio optimization to chemical modeling and machine learning, quantum computing is emerging as a transformative force. This chapter examines the state of quantum computing in commercial settings, outlines key use cases, highlights implementation challenges, and presents strategic pathways for enterprise adoption.

# Enterprise Use Cases for Quantum Computing

## Finance and Risk Modeling

Quantum computing offers powerful tools for simulating financial markets, optimizing investment strategies, and assessing risk under uncertainty. Banks and investment firms can use quantum algorithms such as VQE and QAOA to explore portfolios in high-dimensional spaces and to solve Monte Carlo simulations faster and with more nuance.

### Diagram 1: Quantum Portfolio Optimization Workflow

Financial Dataset → Classical Preprocessing → Quantum Cost Function → VQE/QAOA Solver → Optimized Portfolio

## Supply Chain and Logistics

Companies like DHL, FedEx, and Volkswagen are experimenting with quantum-enhanced optimization techniques to streamline complex logistics networks. Quantum systems are used to:

- Optimize delivery routes

- Predict maintenance schedules

- Manage dynamic inventory under fluctuating demand conditions

Quantum annealing and hybrid solvers provide the foundation for tackling these combinatorial optimization problems.

## Materials and Drug Discovery

Quantum simulations allow researchers to precisely model molecular structures and chemical reactions. This reduces the cost and time associated with trial-and-error lab work in material science and pharmaceutical development.

- **Pharmaceuticals**: Simulate drug interactions at the quantum level.

- **Materials**: Discover novel compounds, superconductors, or nanomaterials using quantum chemistry algorithms.

## Machine Learning and AI

Quantum machine learning (QML) integrates quantum subroutines into traditional models, particularly useful in areas like fraud detection, image classification, and recommendation systems. Quantum kernels and parametric circuits provide new ways to encode, transform, and learn from data.

**Diagram 2: Hybrid Quantum Machine Learning Pipeline**

Raw Data → Classical Feature Extraction → Quantum Embedding → Quantum Circuit Processing → Classical Interpretation

**Energy Sector**

Quantum computing helps energy companies improve efficiency and sustainability. Use cases include:

- Optimizing exploration and drilling

- Modeling molecular interactions in fuel development

- Predictive maintenance and energy distribution in smart grids

Companies such as BP, ExxonMobil, and Shell have invested in quantum R&D for these applications.

---

# Quantum-as-a-Service (QaaS) Business Model

Cloud-based platforms enable businesses to access quantum computing resources without investing in expensive infrastructure. Quantum-as-a-Service (QaaS) provides:

- Remote access to real quantum hardware

- Simulation environments for prototyping

- Developer tools and APIs for application integration

Leading platforms include:

- **IBM Quantum Experience**

- **Amazon Braket**

- **Microsoft Azure Quantum**

- **Google Cloud Quantum Service**

**Diagram 3: Quantum-as-a-Service Interaction Model**

User Interface → Quantum SDK → Cloud API → Backend Processor → Results Returned

QaaS lowers the barrier to experimentation and allows enterprises to develop quantum solutions iteratively.

## Barriers to Commercial Adoption

Despite its potential, quantum computing faces several barriers to broader industry integration:

1. **Scalability** – Most current devices lack the qubit counts or coherence needed for commercial-scale applications.

2. **Talent Shortage** – A limited pool of professionals trained in quantum programming and theory slows adoption.

3. **High Costs** – Both hardware development and access to cloud-based systems entail high financial investment.

4. **Integration Complexity** – Bridging quantum and classical workflows requires robust middleware, data translation layers, and skilled system architects.

5. **Uncertainty of ROI** – Many quantum use cases remain experimental, making business justification difficult without demonstrable value.

---

## Industry Examples and Partnerships

Real-world engagement is growing through partnerships and proof-of-concept studies:

- **JP Morgan and IBM**: Collaborating on quantum finance algorithms.

- **Volkswagen and D-Wave/Google**: Exploring traffic optimization using quantum routing.

- **Roche and Boehringer Ingelheim**: Working with quantum startups on molecular modeling.

- **ExxonMobil**: Using quantum chemistry to study carbon capture and fuel refinement.

These partnerships underscore the strategic nature of early investment in quantum innovation.

---

## Strategic Roadmaps

Many businesses are adopting a staged quantum engagement model:

- **Phase 1**: Build internal quantum literacy, run workshops, train staff, and evaluate use cases.

- **Phase 2**: Develop and test quantum algorithms via cloud platforms using simulators and small devices.

- **Phase 3**: Gradually integrate quantum solutions into classical enterprise systems for hybrid workflows.

- **Phase 4**: Full-scale deployment once hardware and algorithms mature.

Such roadmaps allow companies to build institutional knowledge while preparing for scalable quantum integration.

---

## Conclusion

Quantum computing in business is transitioning from novelty to necessity. While full-scale, fault-tolerant quantum devices may still be a few years away, industry leaders are actively preparing. Enterprises that build in-house expertise, establish quantum strategies, and form external partnerships today are positioning themselves for future success. As hardware improves and software matures, quantum computing will become a critical part of the digital transformation agenda across industries.

---

## Glossary for Chapter 8

- **Quantum-as-a-Service (QaaS)** – A cloud-based delivery model where quantum computing resources are accessed via API.

- **QAOA (Quantum Approximate Optimization Algorithm)** – An algorithm used in solving combinatorial optimization problems.

- **VQE (Variational Quantum Eigensolver)** – A hybrid quantum-classical algorithm useful in finding ground state energies in molecules.

- **Quantum Machine Learning (QML)** – The use of quantum computing to accelerate machine learning algorithms.

- **Quantum Embedding** – A technique in QML where classical data is encoded into quantum states.

- **Quantum Simulator** – Software that mimics quantum circuit behavior on classical computers.

- **Hybrid Architecture** – A computational setup that combines classical processors with quantum accelerators.

- **Quantum Optimization** – The use of quantum methods to solve optimization problems more efficiently than classical methods.

- **Quantum Chemistry** – A domain of chemistry using quantum algorithms to simulate atomic interactions and molecular structures.

- **Quantum-Classical Pipeline** – A system where parts of an algorithm are executed on quantum hardware and others on classical machines.

# Chapter 9

# Ethical and Societal Implications of Quantum Computing

Quantum computing has emerged as one of the most transformative technologies of the 21st century, promising unprecedented computational capabilities and paradigm-shifting innovations. However, with great power comes significant responsibility. As with other disruptive technologies, quantum computing brings with it a range of ethical dilemmas, societal repercussions, and philosophical inquiries. This chapter explores these complex issues in depth, from global access and technological inequality to surveillance risks, labor disruption, and moral philosophy. As nations, corporations, and institutions race toward quantum advantage, thoughtful reflection and proactive planning are crucial to ensuring its benefits are equitable, sustainable, and aligned with human values.

## Economic Inequality and Global Access

As quantum computing advances, it risks exacerbating global disparities in technological access and innovation capacity. Quantum infrastructure—relying on cryogenic systems, advanced materials, and elite research teams—remains concentrated in high-income countries and elite research institutions.

**Diagram 1: Quantum Access Disparity**

High-Income Countries: Hardware, R&D, Cloud Access
Low-Income Countries : Limited Access, Dependency on Foreign Systems

The result may be a deepening digital divide, with economically disadvantaged nations dependent on foreign quantum services, unable to fully participate in the next era of computational discovery, security infrastructure, or innovation economies. Addressing this divide requires global cooperation in training, open-access frameworks, and public-private partnerships.

## Privacy and Surveillance

The encryption methods that underpin today's digital society are at risk of becoming obsolete due to the capabilities of quantum computers. This introduces unprecedented threats to privacy, not only for future communications but also for encrypted data harvested today.

- Medical records, biometric identities, and genomic data

- Financial transactions and legal documents

- Confidential business intelligence and strategic research

Moreover, authoritarian regimes and private surveillance companies could leverage quantum decryption capabilities to exert disproportionate control, perform mass surveillance, or undermine geopolitical opponents. Legislative safeguards and ethical norms will need to evolve quickly to protect civil liberties in a post-quantum world.

# Ethical AI and Quantum Machine Learning

Quantum computing enhances artificial intelligence by enabling the processing of high-dimensional data with quantum speedups. However, these hybrid quantum-AI systems inherit the opacity and unpredictability of both domains.

Ethical concerns include:

- **Bias Amplification**: Poorly calibrated training data may propagate discriminatory outputs.

- **Autonomy and Accountability**: Quantum-AI agents may act beyond human understanding, making accountability difficult.

- **Security Risks**: AI-driven quantum systems used in cyberwarfare, finance, or medical diagnostics could cause widespread harm if misapplied.

**Diagram 2: Quantum-AI Feedback Loop**

Quantum Data Processing → Model Training → Automated Decision → Ethical Oversight → Model Refinement

Transparency, interpretability, and accountability mechanisms must be prioritized alongside performance gains.

## Philosophical Implications

Quantum computing raises profound philosophical questions, not only in physics but also in metaphysics, epistemology, and philosophy of mind.

Key philosophical challenges include:

- **Nature of Reality**: Quantum entanglement and superposition blur the distinction between determinism and probability.

- **Observer Effect**: The act of measurement in quantum systems revives debates about the role of consciousness.

- **Information Ontology**: What does it mean for information to be non-local or retrocausal in entangled systems?

These questions invite collaboration between philosophers and scientists to explore how our evolving understanding of computation affects broader human inquiry.

---

## Labor Displacement and Workforce Transformation

Quantum disruption will affect the workforce through

automation of complex problem-solving tasks, optimization routines, and scientific modeling.

Sectors most at risk include:

- Financial risk modeling

- Chemical and pharmaceutical research

- Cybersecurity and encryption services

To mitigate displacement, governments and educators must:

- Launch quantum literacy initiatives

- Fund interdisciplinary training programs

- Promote inclusion in STEM and quantum fields

Workforce evolution will be as critical as technological evolution in determining the societal success of quantum adoption.

## Policy and Regulation

Global quantum governance is in its infancy, but momentum is building. Regulatory frameworks must address:

- **Export Controls**: Restricting sensitive quantum hardware and software.

- **Ethical Standards**: Establishing boundaries for use in

surveillance, AI, and military operations.

- **Cross-Border Collaboration**: Developing norms for quantum research, communication, and conflict prevention.

- **Quantum Transparency**: Ensuring public accountability in the deployment of quantum infrastructure.

International collaboration through entities such as the United Nations, ITU, or WEF will be essential to harmonize policies and prevent fragmentation.

---

## Conclusion

Quantum computing offers unparalleled potential but demands thoughtful stewardship. The path forward requires more than technical mastery—it necessitates ethical foresight, inclusive planning, and robust public dialogue. By embedding ethical frameworks and human-centric values into the development of quantum technologies, we can ensure they uplift humanity rather than deepen existing divides. The quantum age is as much a moral evolution as it is a technological revolution.

# Glossary for Chapter 9

- **Quantum Ethics** – The field of ethics concerned with the moral implications of quantum technologies.

- **Quantum Inequality** – Disparity in access to quantum resources and education.

- **Quantum-AI Integration** – The use of quantum computing to enhance machine learning and decision-making.

- **Post-Quantum Surveillance** – Potential surveillance practices made possible by breaking current encryption through quantum means.

- **Quantum-Ready Regulation** – Policies and legal frameworks designed to address the implications of quantum computing.

- **Entangled Information** – Quantum information that exhibits non-local correlations due to entanglement.

- **Quantum Labor Market** – The set of emerging careers and educational pathways related to quantum technologies.

- **Retroactive Decryption** – The risk that data encrypted today could be broken in the future by quantum computers.

# Chapter 10

# The Future of Quantum Computing

Quantum computing has transitioned from theoretical exploration to experimental reality and is approaching the threshold of practical application. As the field matures, attention increasingly turns to its long-term trajectory: how quantum technologies will evolve, integrate into broader computational ecosystems, and reshape society in the coming decades. This final chapter offers a forward-looking synthesis of trends, challenges, and possibilities that define the future of quantum computing.

## Hardware Scalability and Fault Tolerance

The next frontier in quantum hardware is scalability—constructing systems with hundreds of thousands or even millions of qubits that can operate reliably. This includes:

- **Quantum Error Correction (QEC)**: Creating robust error-correcting codes like the surface code or cat code to combat decoherence.

- **Modular Quantum Architectures**: Linking smaller quantum modules to create large-scale networks.

- **Cryogenic and Photonic Systems**: Reducing noise through extreme cooling or using room-temperature photonic approaches.

**Diagram 1: Future Hardware Evolution Path**

Prototype Devices → NISQ Processors → Error-Corrected Nodes → Scalable Modular Systems

## Software Ecosystem Maturation

As hardware matures, the software stack must evolve in tandem. Key trends include:

- **High-Level Languages**: Platforms like Qiskit, Cirq, and Q# will be abstracted further for accessibility.

- **Cross-Platform Toolkits**: Tools allowing seamless code portability between devices.

- **Hybrid Frameworks**: Tight integration between CPUs, GPUs, and quantum processors.

- **AI-Augmented Development**: Use of machine learning to improve quantum circuit optimization.

**Diagram 2: Quantum Software Stack (Future Projection)**

User Interface → Middleware → Compiler Layer → Hardware-Specific Interface → QPU

# Quantum Internet and Communication

Long-term visions for the quantum internet focus on ultra-secure communications and distributed quantum computing:

- **Entanglement Distribution**: Secure communication via entangled states shared between distant nodes.

- **Quantum Repeaters**: Enabling signal regeneration and long-distance entanglement.

- **Quantum Cloud Platforms**: Hosting and accessing remote quantum services.

**Diagram 3: Future Quantum Internet Topology**

Node A ↔ Quantum Repeater ↔ Node B ↔ Quantum Processor Cloud ↔ User

## Global Strategy and Policy

Governments will play a pivotal role in shaping the quantum future through:

- **Quantum Investment Initiatives**: Continued public funding for infrastructure, education, and research.

- **International Standards**: Agreements on interoperability, ethics, and security.

- **Quantum Diplomacy**: Cooperation to avoid technological hegemony and promote shared benefits.

Examples include:

- U.S. National Quantum Initiative

- EU Quantum Flagship

- China's National Quantum Laboratory

## Ethical and Educational Evolution

Preparing the global population for quantum impact will require massive education and outreach:

- **Curriculum Integration**: Quantum topics embedded into K–12 and university programs.

- **Interdisciplinary Research**: Combining physics, engineering, computer science, and ethics.

- **Public Engagement**: Explaining risks and opportunities to non-specialists.

Additionally, ensuring access across socio-economic lines will be critical to avoid a "quantum divide."


## Vision for the Next 20–50 Years

Looking further ahead, we may see:

- **Consumer Quantum Devices**: Personal quantum accelerators embedded in home systems.

- **Quantum-AI Agents**: Cognitive systems that reason across vast datasets using quantum-enhanced AI.

- **Quantum Sensors**: Tools for geology, biology, and defense that leverage entanglement and superposition.

- **Decentralized Quantum Networks**: Quantum blockchain or smart contracts powered by entanglement.

**Diagram 4: Quantum Integration into Society (Long-Term)**

Quantum AI → Health Diagnostics

Quantum Sensors → Environmental Monitoring

Quantum Networks → Global Infrastructure

---

# Conclusion

The future of quantum computing is bright but complex. It encompasses a convergence of disciplines, demands a new generation of thinkers, and invites global collaboration. With foresight and ethical foresight, quantum technologies can enable breakthroughs across industries, sciences, and even the structure of human knowledge.

# Glossary for Chapter 10

- **Quantum Repeater** – A device that enables long-distance entanglement for quantum communication.

- **Quantum Internet** – A proposed network that uses quantum signals to transmit information securely.

- **Quantum Diplomacy** – The use of international policy and cooperation to regulate and promote equitable quantum development.

- **Quantum AI Agent** – An autonomous system combining quantum computing and artificial intelligence.

- **Decentralized Quantum Network** – A distributed quantum system designed for secure, tamper-proof operations.

- **Modular Quantum Architecture** – A scalable approach that connects smaller quantum systems into a larger computational unit.

- **Quantum Software Stack** – The layered software environment that enables programming and executing quantum algorithms.

- **Surface Code** – A quantum error-correcting code using 2D qubit arrangements to protect information.

- **Quantum Cloud** – A model in which quantum computing resources are accessed remotely via the internet.

- **Quantum Sensor** – A device using quantum effects to make high-precision measurements.

# References and Supporting Materials

- Arute, F., et al. (2019). Quantum supremacy using a programmable superconducting processor. *Nature*, 574(7779), 505–510.

- Bostrom, N. (2014). *Superintelligence: Paths, Dangers, Strategies*. Oxford University Press.

- Deutsch, D. (1985). Quantum theory, the Church–Turing principle and the universal quantum computer. *Proceedings of the Royal Society A*, 400(1818), 97–117.

- Floridi, L. (2013). *The Ethics of Information*. Oxford University Press.

- Feynman, R. P. (1982). Simulating physics with computers. *International Journal of Theoretical Physics*, 21(6–7), 467–488.

- Grover, L. K. (1996). A fast quantum mechanical algorithm for database search. *Proceedings of the 28th Annual ACM Symposium on Theory of Computing*, 212–219.

- McArdle, S., Endo, S., Aspuru-Guzik, A., et al. (2020). Quantum computational chemistry. *Reviews of Modern Physics*, 92(1), 015003.

- Montanaro, A. (2016). Quantum algorithms: An overview. *npj Quantum Information*, 2, 15023.

- National Academies of Sciences, Engineering, and Medicine. (2019). *Quantum Computing: Progress and Prospects*. National Academies Press.

- Nielsen, M. A., & Chuang, I. L. (2010). *Quantum Computation and Quantum Information* (10th anniversary ed.). Cambridge University Press.

- Orús, R., Mugel, S., & Lizaso, E. (2019). Quantum computing for finance: Overview and prospects. *Reviews in Physics*, 4, 100028.

- Perdomo-Ortiz, A., Benedetti, M., Realpe-Gomez, J., & Biswas, R. (2018). Opportunities and challenges for quantum-assisted machine learning in near-term quantum computers. *Quantum Science and Technology*, 3(3), 030502.

- Preskill, J. (2018). Quantum Computing in the NISQ era and beyond. *Quantum*, 2, 79.

- Shor, P. W. (1994). Algorithms for quantum

computation: Discrete logarithms and factoring. *Proceedings of the 35th Annual Symposium on Foundations of Computer Science*, 124–134.

- UNESCO. (2022). *Global Digital Ethics Framework.*

- U.S. Department of Commerce. (2023). *Quantum Export Controls Policy Brief.*

- Venturelli, D., et al. (2015). Quantum optimization of fully connected spin glasses. *Physical Review X*, 5(3), 031040.

- Woerner, S., & Egger, D. J. (2019). Quantum risk analysis. *npj Quantum Information*, 5(1), 15.

- World Economic Forum. (2022). *Quantum Computing Governance Principles.*

- Zeng, Q., et al. (2023). *Ethical Considerations in Quantum-AI Systems.* Journal of Technology Ethics.

*Thank you, I hope you enjoyed this*

*enhanced and updated 2ⁿᵈ Edition*

*Please be sure to read:*

**"QUANTUM PHYSICS FOR THE PRACTICAL MAN"**

*ALSO AVAILABLE ON AMAZON BOOKS AND KINDLE*

www.ingramcontent.com/pod-product-compliance
Lightning Source LLC
LaVergne TN
LVHW051746050326
832903LV00029B/2754